Why Can't I Breathe Underwater?

and other questions about the respiratory system

by

Sharon Cromwell

Photographs by

Richard Smolinski, Jr.

Series Consultant

Dan Hogan

RIGBY INTERACTIVE LIBRARY
DES PLAINES, ILLINOIS

© 1998 Reed Educational & Professional Publishing
Published by Rigby Interactive Library,
an imprint of Reed Educational & Professional Publishing,
1350 East Touhy Avenue, Suite 240 West
Des Plaines, IL 60018

02 01 00 99 98
10 9 8 7 6 5 4 3 2 1

Cover photo, pages 10–11, 22: © George Kamper/Tony Stone Images

Produced by Times Offset (M) Sdn. Bhd.

Library of Congress Cataloging-in-Publication Data

Cromwell, Sharon, 1947-
    Why can't I breathe underwater? : and other questions about the respiratory system / by Sharon Cromwell ; photographs by Richard Smolinski, Jr.
    p.   cm. -- (Bodywise)
    Includes bibliographical references and index.
    Summary: Describes how the human respiratory system works and discusses such related topics as yawning, hiccuping, and coughing.
    ISBN 1-57572-158-9 (lib. bdg.)
    1. Respiratory organs--Physiology--Juvenile literature.
[1. Respiratory system.]   I. Smolinski, Dick, ill. II. Title. III. Series.
QP121.C79   1997
612.2--dc21

                             97-22212
                                CIP
                                AC

Some words are shown in bold, **like this.** You can find out what they mean by looking in the glossary.

Contents

What is my respiratory system?

Do you know what happens to air after you breathe it in? Air enters your nose or mouth. It also enters your body through your skin. Air goes from your nose or mouth into your **windpipe**. This is a tube in your chest. Then it goes into your two lungs.

Oxygen is a **gas** in air. It is **absorbed** into your lungs. From there, oxygen goes through the walls of your lungs into the blood **cells** in your blood vessels. These are tiny tubes that carry blood around in your body. Blood cells carry oxygen to every cell in your body.

HEALTH FACT
Without oxygen, your body cannot function, or do its work.

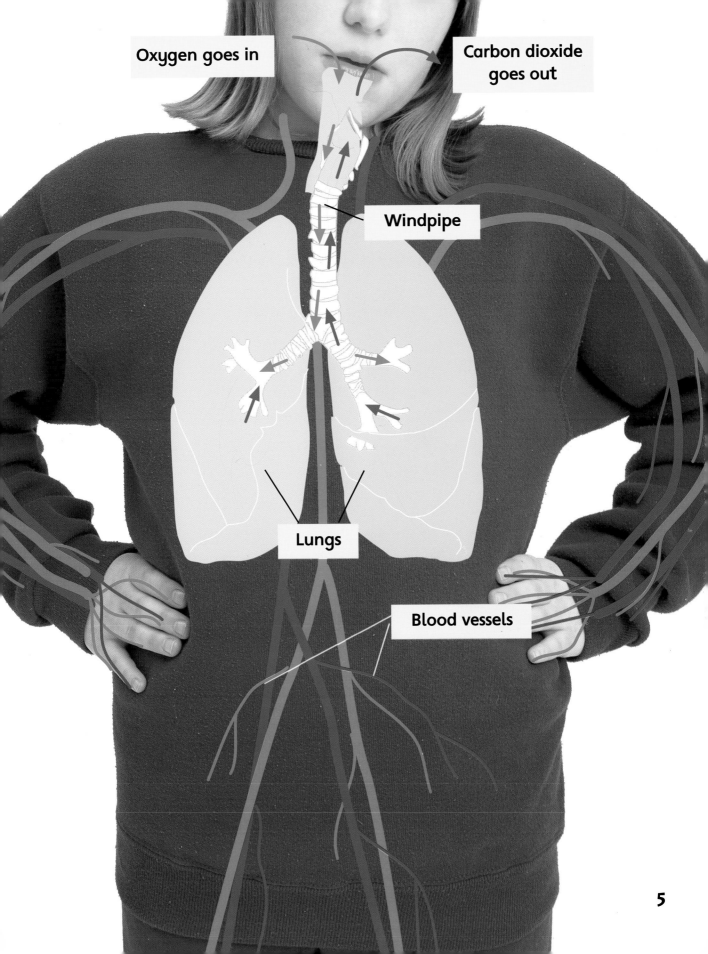

Oxygen goes in

Carbon dioxide goes out

Windpipe

Lungs

Blood vessels

5

What happens to the oxygen I breathe in?

Energy keeps your body alive and working. Energy from food you have **digested** is in your **cells**. **Oxygen** helps to release that energy so it can be used as fuel by your body. When energy is released, a **gas** called carbon dioxide is also released. Blood cells in blood vessels carry carbon dioxide back to your lungs as **waste**. The waste then passes back through the walls of your lungs. The carbon dioxide then leaves your body when you breathe out.

HEALTH FACT

When you blow up a balloon, you are filling it with carbon dioxide.

Why do I breathe in and out?

You breathe in to get **oxygen** from the air. You breathe out to get rid of **waste gas** called carbon dioxide.

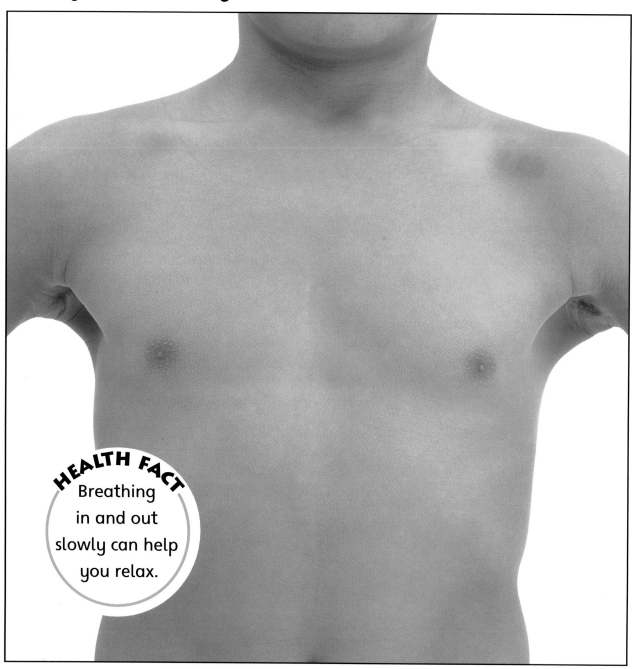

HEALTH FACT
Breathing in and out slowly can help you relax.

1. Both your lungs work the same way. They take in oxygen from the air you breathe.

2. Your lungs and your heart work together. Your heart is a muscle. When it squeezes together, it pumps blood around your body.

Lung

Lung

Heart

3. You heart's pumping helps blood cells move through your body. Your blood **cells** carry the oxygen that you have breathed in.

4. Other blood cells carry carbon dioxide back through the body to your lungs. From the lungs, carbon dioxide is breathed out of the body.

9

Why can't I breathe underwater?

Your lungs need to breathe in a **gas,** not a liquid.

HEALTH FACT

If you learn to swim well, you will build up strong lungs.

- If you breathe underwater, the water will enter your **windpipe** and will fill up your lungs. Water is a liquid.

- Only gases like **oxygen** and carbon dioxide can move through your lungs.

- A liquid like water cannot move through your lungs fast enough for you to breathe.

- If you cannot breathe, you cannot **survive**.

What happens to my breathing when I sleep?

When you sleep, your breathing slows down.

HEALTH FACT

A good night's sleep gives you energy, helps you to learn, and makes you feel good.

1. As you sleep, your muscles relax.

2. When they are relaxed, your muscles need less energy and **oxygen**.

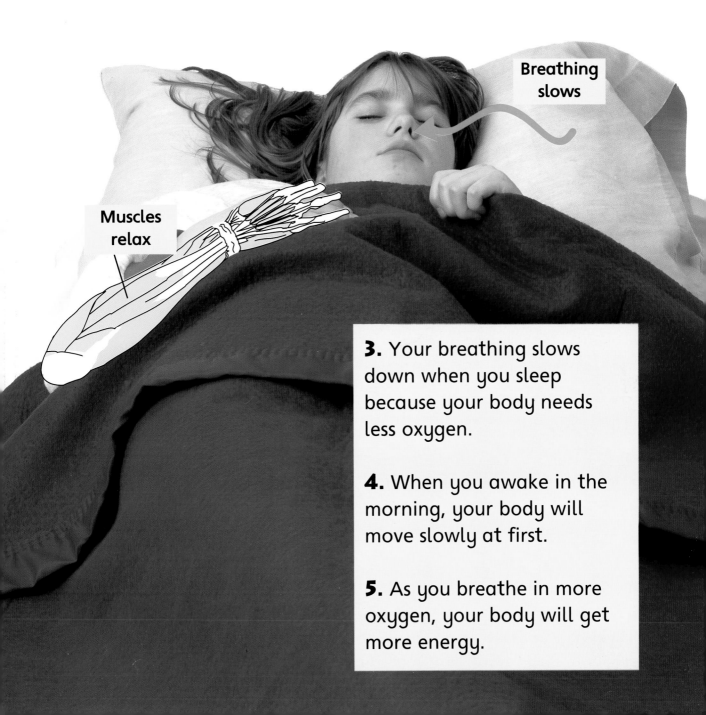

Breathing slows

Muscles relax

3. Your breathing slows down when you sleep because your body needs less oxygen.

4. When you awake in the morning, your body will move slowly at first.

5. As you breathe in more oxygen, your body will get more energy.

Why do I yawn?

Yawning gives your body a big dose of **oxygen**.

HEALTH FACT

Trees and plants make the air around us healthier because they give off oxygen.

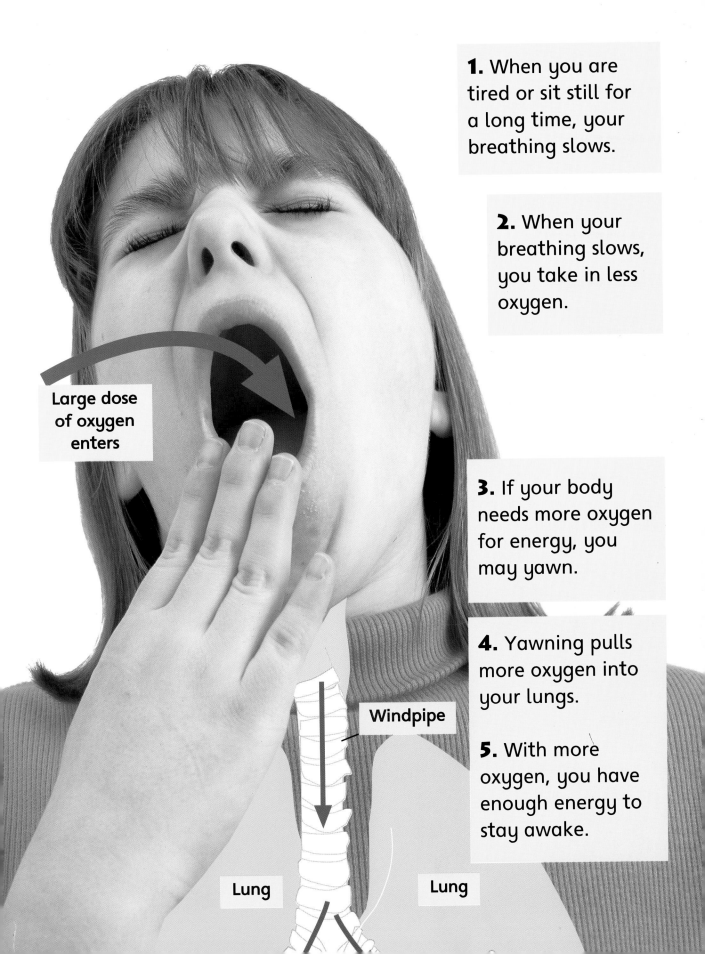

1. When you are tired or sit still for a long time, your breathing slows.

2. When your breathing slows, you take in less oxygen.

Large dose of oxygen enters

3. If your body needs more oxygen for energy, you may yawn.

4. Yawning pulls more oxygen into your lungs.

Windpipe

5. With more oxygen, you have enough energy to stay awake.

Lung

Lung

Why do I breathe hard after playing basketball?

You need more **oxygen** to use more energy.

HEALTH FACT
When you exercise, your heart beats about 150 times a minute! Regular exercise helps your heart to function better.

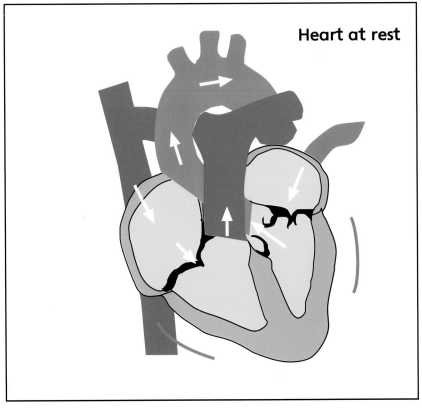

Heart at rest

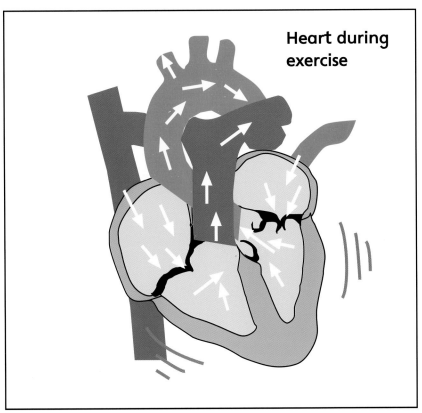

Heart during exercise

1. While running and jumping, you use up oxygen faster than it can be replaced by regular breathing.

2. So you need a lot more oxygen to get more energy when you play basketball.

3. You breathe hard to take in more oxygen. Your heart pumps faster in order to get this oxygen to the parts of your body.

4. With more oxygen, you release energy faster. This helps you have energy to play basketball.

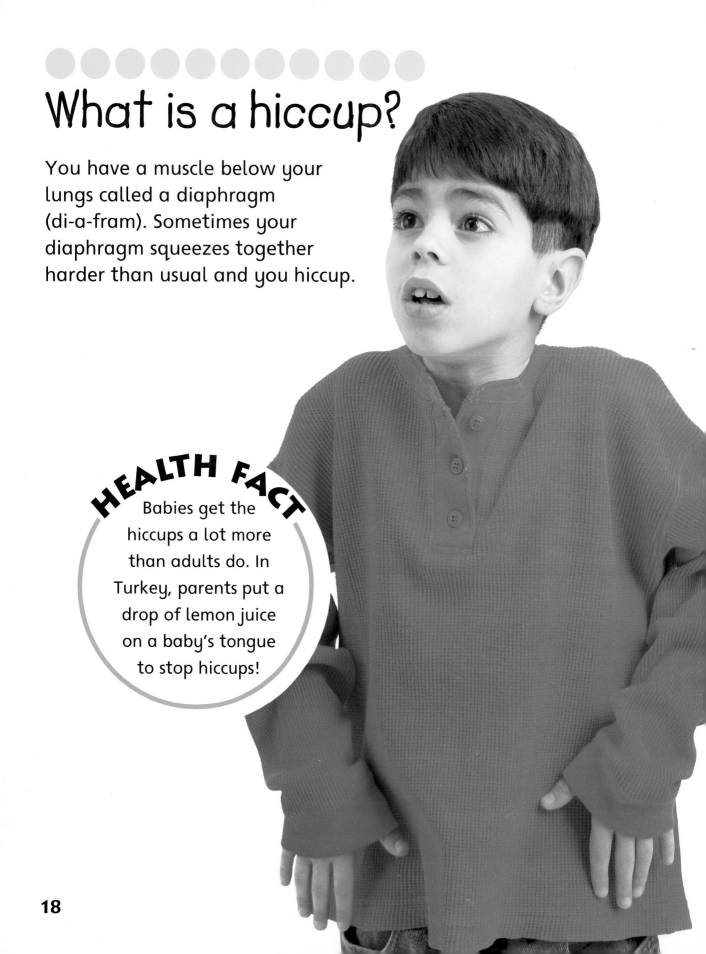

What is a hiccup?

You have a muscle below your lungs called a diaphragm (di-a-fram). Sometimes your diaphragm squeezes together harder than usual and you hiccup.

HEALTH FACT

Babies get the hiccups a lot more than adults do. In Turkey, parents put a drop of lemon juice on a baby's tongue to stop hiccups!

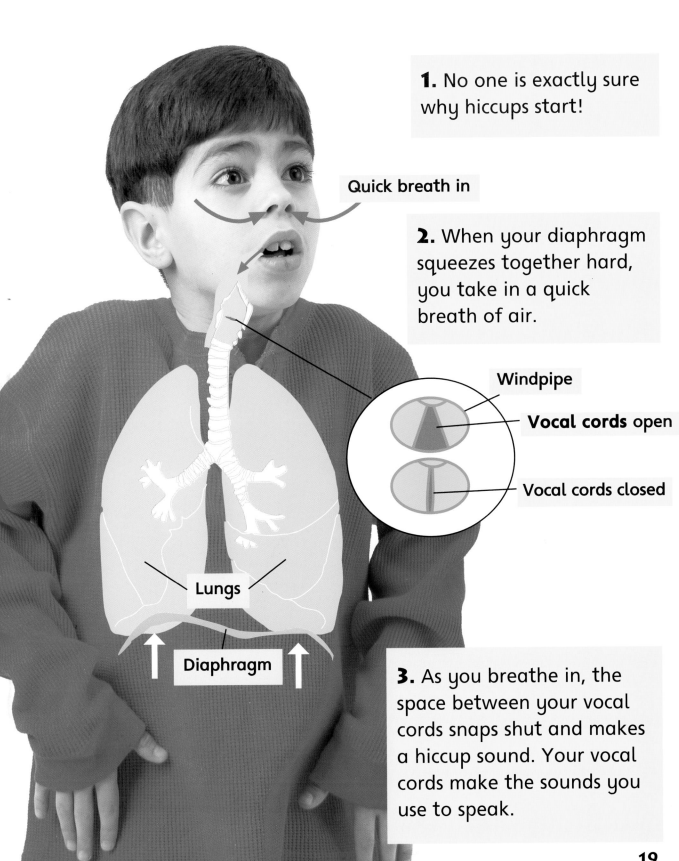

1. No one is exactly sure why hiccups start!

Quick breath in

2. When your diaphragm squeezes together hard, you take in a quick breath of air.

Windpipe

Vocal cords open

Vocal cords closed

Lungs

Diaphragm

3. As you breathe in, the space between your vocal cords snaps shut and makes a hiccup sound. Your vocal cords make the sounds you use to speak.

19

Why do I cough?

Coughing is your body's way of pushing out unwanted substances.

HEALTH FACT

Smoking is bad for your lungs. Over time, it makes it harder for your lungs to **absorb oxygen**.

1. Your throat and **windpipe** are coated with a slimy substance called mucus. Mucus helps to trap tiny bits of dust and other unwanted things.

2. If too many tiny bits get into the mucus in your throat or windpipe, you cough.

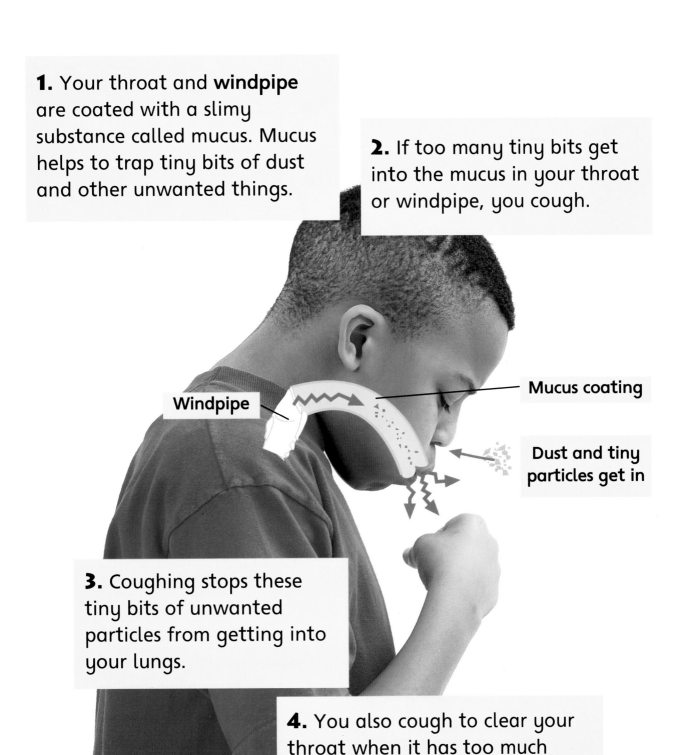

Mucus coating

Windpipe

Dust and tiny particles get in

3. Coughing stops these tiny bits of unwanted particles from getting into your lungs.

4. You also cough to clear your throat when it has too much mucus in it. This can happen when you have a cold.

EXPLORE MORE!
Your Respiratory System

1. IT'S BREATHTAKING!
WHAT YOU'LL NEED:
- A sports watch or clock with a second hand
- A quiet place
- A friend to help you

THEN TRY THIS!
Relax, sit quietly for 1 minute. Breathe normally. Count how many times you breathe. Have your friend time you with a sports watch and tell you when 1 minute is over. Write down how many times you breathed. Now jog in the same spot for 1 minute. Count how many times you breathe. Again, have your friend time you and tell you when 1 minute is over. Write down how many times you breathed. How many breaths did you take while sitting still? How many breaths did you take

while jogging in place? Did you take more breaths doing one thing than doing the other?

2. HICCUP HELP!
WHAT YOU'LL NEED:
- A glass of water
- A balloon
- A friend to help you

THEN TRY THIS!

The next time you get the hiccups, try one or more of the most common home cures:
1) Drink a glass of water while holding your nose.
2) Stand on your head for about 2 minutes.
3) Have a friend startle you.
4) Blow up a balloon.

3 MIRROR, MIRROR
WHAT YOU'LL NEED:
• A mirror

THEN TRY THIS!

Hold your mouth about 2 inches from a mirror. Breathe out onto the mirror a few times. What happens? When you breathe out, you **exhale** carbon dioxide and water. What do these two

things do to the mirror? Can you see water on the mirror after a few breaths?

4. TREASURE CHEST
WHAT YOU'LL NEED:
• A long, thin strip of paper
• Tape

THEN TRY THIS!

Tape the strip of paper snugly around your chest. Take a deep breath in. Can you breathe in enough to pop the paper strip? Your chest expands as you breathe in and your lungs fill up with air.

Glossary

absorbed Sucked up or taken up.

cells Very small parts of a person, animal, or plant.

digested Broken down into parts your body can use or get rid of.

exhale Breathe out.

gas A substance, such as air, that spreads to fill the space it is in.

oxygen A colorless **gas** that is in the air. We need oxygen to breathe.

survive To continue to live.

vocal cords The ridges in the voice box, which is in your throat. These ridges help you speak.

waste Something your body doesn't need.

windpipe A pipe in the throat that air passes through on the way to the lungs.

More Books to Read

Bailey, Donna. *All About Your Lungs.* Chatham, NJ: Raintree Steck-Vaughn, 1990.

Ganeri, Anita. *Breathing.* Chatham, NJ: Raintree Steck-Vaughn, 1990.

Lungs and Breathing. Morristown, NJ: Silver Burdett Press, 1988.

Parker, Steve. *The Lungs and Breathing.* Danbury, CT: Franklin Watts, 1991.

Suhr, Mandy. *How I Breathe.* Minneapolis, MN: Lerner Group, 1992.

Index